The Pup Sniffed Too Much

Written by Claire Llewellyn
Illustrated by Mike Gordon

Harcourt
Supplemental Publishers

Rigby • Steck-Vaughn

www.steck-vaughn.com

Nina and Chimp were playing at home.

Dad came in with a box.

He said, "Come see what is in the box."

Nina looked in the box.

There was a puppy!

The puppy sniffed Nina.

He sniffed Dad.

He sniffed Chimp.

Then he sniffed Nina again!

4

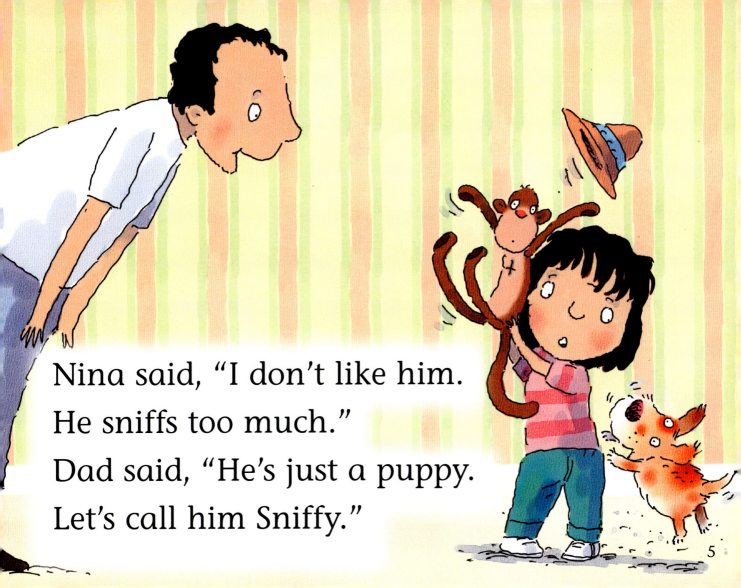

Nina said, "I don't like him.
He sniffs too much."
Dad said, "He's just a puppy.
Let's call him Sniffy."

5

Nina and Chimp were playing on the bed.
Sniffy wanted to play, too.

He sniffed Nina.

He sniffed the bed.

He sniffed Chimp.

Then he sniffed Nina again!

Nina said, "I still don't like him.
He sniffs too much."
Dad said, "He's just a puppy."

8

The next day, Nina and Dad went to the park.
They took Chimp and Sniffy.
Nina and Chimp were playing on the swings.
Sniffy wanted to play, too.

He sniffed Nina.

He sniffed the swings.

He sniffed Chimp.

Then he sniffed Nina again!

"I still don't like Sniffy," Nina said.

"He sniffs too much."

"He's just a puppy," Dad said.

The next day, Nina was playing at home.

She wanted Chimp.

She could not find him!

Nina looked for Chimp.

Sniffy wanted to look, too.

He sniffed the bed.

He sniffed the box.

But he could not find Chimp.

13

Dad said, "Let's go to the park.
Let's see if we can find Chimp there."

Dad and Nina looked for Chimp at the park.
They did not see Chimp.

What did Sniffy do?
He sniffed Nina.
He sniffed the swing.
He sniffed Chimp!

Nina said, "Dad, Sniffy's just a puppy, but I like him!"